Title VI
District 140

Look What Came From Ireland

by
Miles Harvey

Franklin Watts
A Division of Scholastic Inc.
New York Toronto London Auckland Sydney
Mexico City New Delhi Hong Kong
Danbury, Connecticut

Series Concept: Shari Joffe
Design: Steve Marton

Library of Congress Cataloging-in-Publication Data

Harvey, Miles.
   Look what came from Ireland / by Miles Harvey.
      p. cm. — (Look what came from series)
   Includes bibliographical references and index.
   Summary: Describes the many things that originally came from
Ireland, such as holidays, food, sports, musical instruments, and
fashion. Includes a recipe for Irish soda bread.
   ISBN 0-531-11960-2 (lib. bdg.)   0-531-16628-7 (pbk.)
   1. Ireland—Juvenile literature. [1.Ireland—Civilization.
2. Civilization, Modern—Irish influences.] I. Title. II. Series.
DA906.H36 2001
941.5—dc21

                                                    2001046794

Photographs © 2002: AllSport USA/Getty Images/Billy Stickland: 22;
Archive Photos/Getty Images: 20 top, 32 left; Bill Lynch/www.SetDancing
News.net: 12 right, 12 left; Corbis Images: border 4-32 (Historical Picture
Archive), 18 right, 18 left, 19 left (Yann Arthus-Bertrand), 10 left (Jacqui
Hurst), 4 (Bob Krist), 24 left (Minnesota Historical Society), 15 right,
19 bottom right, 23 bottom, 23 top (Michael St. Maur Sheil), 21 (Tim
Thompson), 25 top right (Patrick Ward); David Manufacture de Harpes:
15 left; Dembinsky Photo Assoc./Greg Gawlowski: cover background; Envision:
8 top left (George Mattei), 11 right, 27 (Steven Needham); Getty Images:
3 (Jean-Marc Giboux), 7 right, 7 left (Chip Hires), 20 bottom (L. Malis),
6 left (Bill Pugliano); Kindra Clineff: 1; Photo Researchers, NY: cover
bottom left, 6 right (Jim Corwin), 25 left (Dennis Flaherty), 17 top (Farrett
Grehan), 18 center right, 18 center left (Carolyn A. McKeone), 19 top right
(Elisabeth Weiland); PhotoEdit/Bonnie Kamin: 13; The Image Works: cover
top left, 25 bottom right (Mark Antman), cover right (John Griffin); Tony
Freeman Photographs: back cover, 8 top right, 8 bottom, 9 bottom, 9 top,
10 right, 11 left, 14, 16 left, 16 right, 17 bottom left, 17 bottom right; Woodfin
Camp & Associates/Momatiuk/Eastcott: 24 right.

Contents

The Emerald Isle

The flag of Ireland

"Emerald" is another word for green. And if you look on a map west of Great Britain, you'll find an island so full of beautiful green plants and fields that it is sometimes known as the Emerald Isle. But that is only a nickname. The real name for this amazing place is Ireland.

Ireland is divided into two parts. The biggest part is an independent country called the Republic of Ireland. The smaller part is known as Northern Ireland, and it has long been ruled by Great Britain. In 1998, the people of both the Republic of Ireland and Northern Ireland voted for new laws that would bring these two parts closer together.

Ireland is only about the size of the state of South Carolina. But although it is a small land, it has had a big impact on the rest of the world. In fact, some of the food we eat, music we listen to, and clothes we wear were created in Ireland. So come on! Let's look at all the cool things that come from Ireland!

Holidays

Jack-o'-lantern

The Irish invented **Halloween** about 2,500 years ago. In those days, the people who lived in Ireland were known as the Celts. Every October 31, Celtic families would light huge bonfires and dress up as witches, goblins, and demons. They did this to frighten away the spirits of the dead.

The ancient Celts also invented jack-o'-lanterns. Originally, these Halloween decorations were made out of turnips. But when lots of Irish people began moving to the United States about 150 years ago, they couldn't find many turnips. So they made their jack-o'-lanterns out of pumpkins instead!

Another holiday that comes from Ireland is Saint Patrick's Day. It is named after a religious leader who lived about 1,600 years ago.

St. Patrick's Day parade in Dublin, Ireland

Today, this holiday celebrates not only St. Patrick but all of Ireland, as well as its people and traditions. In the United States, people whose families originally came from Ireland hold parades and wear green clothing to honor their connection to the Emerald Isle.

People celebrating St. Patrick's Day in Dublin, Ireland

7

Food

Potatoes

Colcannon

Boxty

Although potatoes did not originate in Ireland, they are a well-known staple of the Irish diet. One famous Irish potato dish is **boxty,** a kind of potato pancake.

Another popular Irish dish made from potatoes is **colcannon,** which is mashed potatoes mixed with cabbage or kale. Colcannon is often served at dinner on All Hallows' Eve, the Irish name for Halloween.

Barmbrack is another Irish food traditionally served on Halloween. It's a kind of bread made with delicious fruits and spices. Long ago, people had a special way of telling each other's fortunes using barmbrack. They would stick a golden ring into the dough before the bread went into the oven. According to legend, the person who got the slice of barmbrack with the ring in it would be married within a year.

Barmbrack

more food

Irish Christmas cake

People in Ireland also make a special dessert for Christmas. **Irish Christmas cake** is full of fruits and nuts and is usually covered with marzipan, a frosting made of sugar and ground almonds.

Irish stew is made with lamb, onions, potatoes, and other vegetables. It tastes great on a cold winter day!

Another famous Irish recipe is known as **Dublin coddle.** It is a type of casserole made with pork and potatoes. This dish gets its name from Dublin, Ireland's capital city.

Dublin coddle

Irish stew

A céilí dance

A set dance

Dance

For centuries, people in Ireland have been creating beautiful dances. Now Irish dancing has become popular all over the world, thanks to stage and television shows such as "Riverdance" and "Lord of the Dance."

One kind of Irish dance is a **céilí dance.** Céilí (KAY-lee) dances are group dances,

often performed in a circle or square. In some céilí dances, the dancers stand in two rows, with men on one side and women on the other.

Another popular kind of Irish dancing is **set dancing.** A set dance often involves four couples, and is a little bit like an American square dance.

Step dancing is often performed by just one person. It involves a lot of fancy footwork and is very exciting to watch. In the 1800s,

Step dancers

Irish people brought step dancing with them when they moved to the United States. There, Irish step dancing mixed with dances from Africa and other parts of the world. As a result, whole new styles of dance were created, such as tap dancing and clog dancing.

Musical Intruments

The Irish did not invent bagpipes, but Irish musicians are famous for playing an instrument known as the **uilleann pipes.**

Uilleann (ILL-in) means "elbow." People playing these bagpipes push air through the instrument with a special pump attached to their elbow.

The **Celtic harp** is another very famous Irish instrument. So is the **bodhrán** (BOW-rawn). It is a special drum that is often made from the skin of a goat. It can be played with a stick or by hand. The bodhrán looks easy to play—but it takes a lot more skill than you might think!

Uilleann pipes

Man playing a bodhrán

Celtic harp

Claddagh ring

Fashion

Have you ever heard of a **Claddagh ring?** This unusual ring shows two hands holding a crowned heart, a design that symbolizes love and friendship. According to legend, the first Claddagh ring was made more than 300 years ago by an Irishman who learned to make jewelry after he was kidnapped by pirates. Today, Claddagh rings are said to be the second-best-selling kind of ring in the world.

Only wedding rings are more popular!

The Aran Islands are located just off the western coast of Ireland. The people of these three tiny islands are famous for making a beautiful kind of clothing known as the **Aran sweater.** Today, people from all over the world travel to the islands to buy sweaters.

Another kind of clothing that comes from the Aran Islands is the **crios** (kriss). This handwoven belt is sometimes worn by Irish dancers.

Aran sweater

Crios

The **Irish wolfhound** is the tallest kind of dog in the world. Male Irish wolfhounds can stand as tall as 34 inches (86.4 centimeters)!

The Irish wolfhound is the national dog of Ireland, but it is not the only canine that comes from the Emerald Isle. There's also the **Irish water spaniel.** With its curly, water-repellent fur and funny-looking tail, it is a very unusual animal.

The **Irish terrier** is considered a great guard dog. It is very devoted to human beings. Another popular dog from Ireland is the **Irish setter.**

Animals

Irish water spaniel

Irish terrier

Irish setter

Because Irish setters are so friendly, people all over the world love to have them as pets.

Several types of horses also come from Ireland. The **Irish draught horse** is known for its fantastic jumping ability. Another popular Irish horse is the **Connemara pony.** Because of their small size and friendly personality, these animals make wonderful riding ponies for children.

Irish draught horses

Irish wolfhound

Connemara pony

19

Sports

Illustration of a steeplechase in the 1800s

The Irish love horse racing. In fact, one important type of horse racing, the **steeplechase,** was invented in Ireland in 1752. In a steeplechase, horses have to jump over fences as they race around the track.

People in Ireland enjoy many of the same sports that we do, such as soccer. But they also have some sporting events that are all their own. One of these is **hurling.** It is considered the national pastime of Ireland, and is more than 4,000 years old. In this fast-paced sport, players use curved wooden sticks called *camans* to move a small leather ball toward the other team's goal.

A modern-day steeplechase

A hurling match in Ireland

Another popular Irish sport is **Gaelic football.** In some ways, this game resembles American football. In other ways, it is like soccer. The object of the game is to punch, dribble, or kick the ball into—or over—the other team's goal.

more sports

Gaelic football is a very rough sport, but the Irish also like gentle games, such as **road bowling.** This sport takes place along tiny roads in the Irish countryside.

A Gaelic football match

Road bowling in County Armagh, Northern Ireland

The goal is for each player to get a metal ball from one end
of the course to the other in the smallest number of throws
possible. Sometimes a course can be several miles long.

Ball used in road bowling

23

Words

Most people in Ireland speak English. But many Irish people also speak a very old language called Gaelic (GAY-lik). A lot of words we use all the time have their origins in this beautiful language. For example, have you ever worn **"trousers"?** Sure you have! Trousers are pants.

Trousers

Bog

Leprechaun

A **"bog"** is an area of wet ground. This word probably comes to us from the Gaelic language. So does the word **"loch."** A loch is a lake.

"Leprechaun" is probably one of the most famous Gaelic words. According to Irish legend, a leprechaun is a mischievous, magical spirit who looks like a tiny old man. He owns a pot of gold. He'll tell you where it is—if you can catch him!

Another famous Irish word is **"shamrock."** A shamrock is a kind of clover that grows all over the Emerald Isle. In fact, the shamrock is the national symbol of Ireland.

Loch

Shamrock

A recipe from Ireland

Irish Soda Bread

Have you ever heard of soda bread? No, it's not made from soda pop. But it is yummy. People in Ireland eat it often. Now you can try it too.

You'll need the following ingredients:

- 1 tablespoon of butter or margarine
- 4 cups of all-purpose flour
- 2 teaspoons of baking soda
- 1 teaspoon of cream of tartar
- 1 teaspoon of salt
- 1/4 cup of very fine sugar
- 2 cups of buttermilk
- optional: 1 cup of raisins

You'll also need the following equipment:

- a 9-inch by 5-inch loaf pan
- a large mixing bowl
- a mixing spoon
- a fork
- a measuring cup
- a measuring spoon
- a flour sifter

Before you start, have an adult preheat the oven to 425 degrees. You can do the first part of the recipe yourself, with an adult watching.

1. Wash your hands.
2. Use the butter or margarine to grease the entire inside of the loaf pan.
3. Wash your hands again.
4. Using the measuring cup, put 4 cups of flour into the sifter.

5. Using the measuring spoon, put 2 teaspoons of baking soda, 1 teaspoon of cream of tartar, and 1 teaspoon of salt into the sifter with the flour.
6. Sift the flour, baking soda, cream of tartar, and salt into the mixing bowl. If you don't know how the sifter works, ask an adult to help you.
7. Measure 1/4 cup of sugar and pour it into the bowl. Then take the mixing spoon and mix the sugar in with the other ingredients.
8. Using the mixing spoon, clear a little empty space in the center of the bowl.
9. Measure 2 cups of buttermilk and pour it into the center of the bowl.
10. Using the fork, carefully mix the buttermilk with the rest of the ingredients. Make sure to get rid of all the lumps. You can stop when a soft, smooth dough is formed.
11. Put the dough into the loaf pan.

You'll need an adult to finish up the recipe, but you can help by reading the instructions out loud.

1. Put the bread pan into the oven and bake for 10 minutes.
2. Reduce the heat to 400 degrees.
3. Bake until golden brown and firm to the touch—about 45 minutes.
4. Remove the bread from the oven and let it cool slightly before slicing.

Now you are ready to try Irish soda bread!

How do you say....?

Irish Gaelic is a lovely language that has been spoken by Ireland's Celtic people for thousands of years. Today, Irish Gaelic is the official language of Ireland, along with English. The two languages are very different, though. Try saying a few words, and you'll see why!

English	Irish Gaelic	How to pronounce it
good morning	maidin mhaith	MAH-jin WAH
bye for now	slán go fóill	SLAWN guh FOH-ihll
dog	madra	MAD-ra
drum	druma	DRUM-a
green	glas	glass
horse	capall	KAH-puhl
Halloween	Oíche Shamhna	EE-huh HOW-nuh
potato	práta	PRAY-ta
ring	fáinne	FAWN-yuh

To find out more

Here are some other resources to help you learn more about Ireland:

Books

Arnold, Helen. **Postcards from Ireland.** Raintree/Steck-Vaughn, 1998.

Daly, Ita. **Irish Myths & Legends.** Oxford University Press Children's Books, 2001.

Haskins, Jim and Benson, Kathleen. **Count Your Way Through Ireland.** Carolrhoda Books, 1996.

January, Brendan. **Ireland** (True Books). Children's Press, 1999.

McKay, Patricia. **Ireland** (Festivals of the World). Gareth Stevens, 1998.

Organizations and Online Sites

Blarney Castle
http://www.blarneycastle.ie/index.htm
The official website of a famous Irish castle.

Five-Minute Irish Tales
A collection of 151 short Irish folk tales, some dating back to the 12th century.
http://www.toad.net/~sticker/blackbx.html

Irish Peatland Conservation Council
Find out how bogs are formed, what plants and animals live in them, and how they are being conserved.
http://www.ipcc.ie/factsfigures.html

Irish Tourist Board
345 Park Avenue
New York, NY 10154
http://www.ireland.travel.ie/home/

Map of Ireland
Check out this online map of Ireland, provided by the University of Texas at Austin.
http://www.lib.utexas.edu/maps/europe/ireland.jpg

World Factbook–Ireland
A huge collection of facts about Ireland, compiled by the U.S. government.
http://www.cia.gov/cia/publications/factbook/geos/ei.html

Glossary

bagpipe a musical instrument that consists of a tube, a bag for air, and pipes from which the sound comes

bonfire a large fire built in the open air

canine dog

casserole food baked in a covered dish

emerald brightly or richly green

fortune what will happen to a person in the future

legend an old story that is widely accepted as true but cannot be proved to be so

mischievous showing a spirit of irresponsible playfulness

pastime something that helps to make time pass pleasantly

origin source or cause of something

republic a country whose government is elected by the people

staple something that is a basic part of a person's diet

symbolizes stands for

traditional handed down from generation to generation

turnip a thick white or yellow edible root related to the cabbage

water repellent having a surface that doesn't let water soak into it

Index

Look what doesn't come from Ireland!

St. Patrick

Every year, millions of people around the world celebrate their Irish heritage on Saint Patrick's Day. But **Saint Patrick** himself wasn't actually Irish. He was born in another country—probably England or Wales. When he was 16, he was kidnapped and brought to Ireland to be sold as a slave. Later, he escaped slavery and went on to become a great religious leader.

Meet the Author

Miles Harvey is the author of several books for young people. He lives in Chicago with his wife, Rengin, and his children, Azize and Julian. This book is dedicated to three wonderful boys—Benjamin Doyle, Sam McGrath, and Jackson McGrath—who chased rainbows with Azize on the shores of Ireland's Loch Corrib.